STUDIES IN ENGLISH

General Editor

David Daiches

Already published in the series:

Already published in the series (*continued*):

SHAKESPEARE:
THE TEMPEST

by

JOHN RUSSELL BROWN

*Professor of English in the School of English and
American Studies, University of Sussex*

EDWARD ARNOLD

© JOHN RUSSELL BROWN 1969

First published 1969 by
Edward Arnold (Publishers) Ltd,
41 Bedford Square, London WC1B 3DQ

Reprinted 1972, 1977, 1978, 1982, 1984

ISBN: 0 7131 5463 2

Printed and bound in Great Britain at
The Camelot Press Ltd, Southampton

Contents

General Preface

The object of this series is to provide studies of individual novels, plays and groups of poems and essays which are known to be widely read by students. The emphasis is on clarification and evaluation; biographical and historical facts, while they may be discussed when they throw light on particular elements in a writer's work, are generally subordinated to critical discussion. What kind of work is this? What exactly goes on here? How good is this work, and why? These are the questions that each writer will try to answer.

It should be emphasized that these studies are written on the assumption that the reader has already read carefully the work discussed. The objective is not to enable students to deliver opinions about works they have not read, nor is it to provide ready-made ideas to be applied to works that have been read. In one sense all critical interpretation can be regarded as foisting opinions on readers, but to accept this is to deny the advantages of any sort of critical discussion directed at students or indeed at anybody else. The aim of these studies is to provide what Coleridge called in another context 'aids to reflection' about the works discussed. The interpretations are offered as suggestive rather than as definitive, in the hope of stimulating the reader into developing further his own insights. This is after all the function of all critical discourse among sensible people.

Because of the interest which this kind of study has aroused, it has been decided to extend it first from merely English literature to include also some selected works of American literature and now further to include selected works in English by Commonwealth writers. The criterion will remain that the book studied is important in itself and is widely read by students.

DAVID DAICHES

1. Early Productions and the First Printing of the Play

King James I established a custom of attending the first command performance of a new winter season on Hallowmas or All Saints Day, November 1. For 1611, the play performed in the splendid Banqueting House at Whitehall by the King's Majesty's Servants—the actors' company most popular at court and working under royal privilege and protection—was Shakespeare's *The Tempest*. The same actors had presented another play, the title of which is now lost, on the previous night, and they followed it four nights later with *The Winter's Tale*.

The Banqueting House was chiefly used for performances of royal masques. It could accommodate elaborate scenery designed by Inigo Jones, and was fitted with machinery for transformation scenes, aerial chariots and practicable clouds. In the dances that concluded these entertainments, Prince Henry, the heir to the throne, and his mother, Queen Anne, frequently participated. Orazio Busino, in the service of the Venetian Ambassador, has described this theatre as it was used in January 1618, for Jonson's masque *Pleasure Reconciled to Virtue:*

A large hall is fitted up like a theatre, with well secured boxes all round. The stage is at one end and his Majesty's chair in front under an ample canopy. Near him are stools for the foreign ambassadors . . . . Whilst waiting for the King we amused ourselves by admiring the decorations and beauty of the house with its two orders of columns . . . . The whole is of wood, including even the shafts, which are carved and gilt with much skill. From the roof of these hang festoons and angels in relief with two rows of lights. . . . Although they profess only to admit the favoured ones who are invited, yet every box was filled notably with most noble and richly arrayed ladies, in number some 600 and more according to the general estimate; . . . On [the King] entering the house, the cornets and trumpets to the number of fifteen or twenty began to play very well a sort of recitative. . . . (Venetian State Papers, xv. 111–14).

The Tempest was a most suitable play for such an occasion. Probably this was a first performance at court, for the text is indebted to accounts of a wreck at sea that did not circulate until the autumn of 1610. It is short, and the King did not like long entertainments. It calls for numerous dances, by 'strange shapes', as well as goddesses, water nymphs and sicklemen. It has more cues for song and music than any other of Shakespeare's plays, and requires a *'quaint device'* so that a banquet can disappear as if by magic. A stage direction, *'Juno descends'*, that is linked to a verbal description of her peacocks flying 'amain', gives scope for a flying machine. *The Tempest* indeed—but this is surmise, not scholarly fact—might have been written for court performance, to be acted against scenery like that used for earlier and later masques. Certainly we know that James Maxwell, the Gentleman Usher in charge of the Banqueting House, had spent six days with nine of his assistants preparing for the three plays.

Shakespeare's *Tempest* demands a special attention. Before and after its Hallowmas performance in 1611, it probably took its place in the ordinary repertoire of the King's Men, playing at the Globe Theatre on Bankside and at their more expensive, smaller and enclosed theatre at Blackfriars. But in the preface to his operatic adaptation of the play, *The Enchanted Island* (1674), John Dryden tells us specifically that it 'had formerly been acted with success in the Blackfriars', and it might well have been a particular favourite with the more select audience of this newer theatre. Certainly it was available for a further court performance early in 1613, as part of the celebrations for the marriage of the King's daughter Elizabeth, with Prince Frederick of Bohemia.

When Shakespeare's *Comedies, Histories & Tragedies* were collected in one handsome Folio volume in 1623, seven years after his death, his editors (and fellow actors and sharers in the King's Men), John Hemmings and Henry Condell, put *The Tempest* first of all the plays, and gave it not only pride of place but also a specially prepared text. The manuscript from which the printers worked had probably been written out by Ralph Crane, a scrivener associated with the actors' company for several years previously. Act and scene divisions are clearly marked. Stage-directions are ample and, in suggestions for dress, stage-business and mood, they often seem to be indebted to the author's own notes or an eye-witness account; for example:

Here enters Ariel *before; then* Alonso, *with a frantic gesture, attended by* Gonzalo. . . . Prospero *observing, speaks.*

All entrances are duly provided for, and almost all the exits—a precision seldom found in printed plays at this time. There are remarkably few textual obscurities, and the punctuation is almost pedantic, with many brackets to mark parentheses and a frequent use of colons and semi-colons. All these characteristics make for easy reading and show that unusual care had been taken. (In fact, too much attention has been given, for other texts, like the good quartos of *Hamlet* and *Romeo and Juliet*, tell us that such neatness and detailed consistency owes more to the scribe, and perhaps the editors, than to Shakespeare himself; for *The Tempest*, we have probably lost all trace of Shakespeare's own punctuation.) At the end of the text, a descriptive cast-list is added—with a note on Caliban that is less ambiguous than the many descriptions of this character in the play itself. Quite exceptionally in the Folio as a whole, the location of the action is specified: 'The Scene, an uninhabited Island': this last feature is appropriate to court masques and common in printed versions of them.

For its author, also, *The Tempest* was a very special play. 1605 had probably seen the first performances of *Lear* and *Macbeth*, and three more tragedies followed in the next few years: *Coriolanus, Antony and Cleopatra* and (possibly unfinished and unperformed in Shakespeare's lifetime) *Timon of Athens*. Then, during 1608-10, Shakespeare wrote three plays variously based on romantic narratives: *Pericles*, that may use portions of another man's play; *Cymbeline*, combining Roman, Italian, British and fabulous material; and *The Winter's Tale*, based on a prose romance written twenty years earlier by Robert Greene. *The Tempest* continues and completes this new series: it, too, has gods and enchantments, and court scenes contrasted with pastoral scenes or with plebeian comedy; it provides laughter, sentiment and sensationalism. Its characters, likewise, include a father and his daughter, and they present murderous cunning, lust, chastity and love; its narrative involves separation, reunion, self-examination, fortitude, forgiveness, helplessness, wonder and amazement. But the dramatic style and form of *The Tempest* are very different from those of its predecessors; and it was the last romance, comedy or tragic-comedy—whichever title is chosen for the group—that Shakespeare wrote. It might have been the last play of all.

In the following year, 1612, Shakespeare finished nothing that has survived. In 1613, sometime before June 29, his *Henry VIII* was per-performed. The editors of the First Folio gave this play a place at the end of the earlier *Histories*, but it hardly seems at home there. Many scholars believe that John Fletcher, the new dramatist of the King's Men, had a considerable hand in the writing, contributing whole scenes and inter-polating lines in others.[1] R. A. Foakes, the new Arden editor, argues strongly for Shakespeare's sole authorship; but he acknowledges a considerable influence by Fletcher and suggests that the play was written as a celebration of Princess Elizabeth's wedding. Whatever is the true history of *Henry VIII*, it is incontestable that after this Shakespeare wrote nothing for the stage beyond a part (mostly early in the play) of *The Two Noble Kinsmen* which is largely Fletcher's, and a part, again with Fletcher, of the now lost *Cardenio*. At least we can say that *The Tempest* is Shakespeare's last work largely uninfluenced by the younger dramatist.

The circumstances of Shakespeare's life also mark the particular interest of *The Tempest*. In 1610, the year when he was preparing or writing this play, Shakespeare moved from London to Stratford to live in retirement with his wife at New Place, the house he had purchased thirteen years before and until now had allowed to be partly occupied by his cousin, Thomas Greene. Around his home town, Shakespeare owned a hundred and seven acres of arable land and other property and tithes. His daughter, Judith, probably lived with him until she married in 1616, and the home of his married daughter, Susanna Hall, was a few minutes distant. His will, local records and early tradition, all give evidence of family, friendly and business affairs in and around Stratford until he died on April 23, 1616.

The Tempest presents Prospero, a magician, inhabiting a lonely island with his daughter and attended by spirits and a dispossessed and monstrous islander. At the close of the play the daughter is to be married to a prince and Prospero goes back to Milan, the Dukedom from which he has been deposed. Moreover he breaks his magic staff, drowns his learned books, and frees his chief, airy spirit. Now that his 'charms are all o'erthrown', he speaks an epilogue asking for applause. These

[1] See Cyrus Hoy's article in *Studies in Bibliography*, xv (1962), 76–85.

elements in the play, together with lyrical speeches of renunciation and regret, have led many readers—if not all—to suppose that this is a very personal work, and that in Prospero Shakespeare has written something of himself. A year previously his sonnets had been published for the first time in book form; and these, for all their conscious artifice, give a highly personal impression of the playwright ten and more years earlier.

But *The Tempest* is not a straightforward valediction: in it Shakespeare broke new ground, as well as Prospero his staff. Formally, verbally, scenically, aurally, histrionically, it is packed with innovations. Thematically it reaches far beyond personal issues, and is indebted to wide and up-to-date reading and many years of life and dramatic creation. This last romance is comprehensive, concentrated, complicated; it is a daring, difficult and coolly accomplished experiment; it is also curiously simple. At times it is a very funny play, and sometimes it seems easily or extravagantly beautiful; and yet besides asking for applause, the Epilogue also speaks of failure, barrenness and despair. When Shakespeare wrote *The Tempest* he may well have intended it to be his last play; but nothing is shirked.

2. *The Originality of* The Tempest

(i) *Sources*

Before Shakespeare started to write a play he usually had found a story in prose that awakened his imagination, and this he kept at his side until the work was done. He would read other versions of the same story and refer to them throughout the composition of his own dramatic retelling. Sometimes he would fix on a story in verse or, less often, an old play as the basis for his own invention. Frequently two, three or more, quite different stories were linked together, as contrasts or complements, by Shakespeare's creative mind. For almost all the plays there is a known 'source', or 'sources'; a novel like *Rosalynde*, or the English histories, or Plutarch's *Lives*, or Arthur Brooke's poem *Romeus and Juliet*. But *The Tempest* has not yielded its secret.

If the text of this play were newly discovered today, scholars would at once be busy searching for its source; and although by now every word has been carefully studied, the search for a source still goes on. For the action of *The Tempest* is not unusual in its detail. A miraculous escape at sea, the separation and rivalry of brothers, a magician exerting his power over enemies, a prince wooing an unknown maiden later discovered to be of royal blood: all these were stock incidents of Renaissance narrative romance. The deposition of a duke and a plot to kill a king were common and significant in both fact and fiction. Taken out of context, the incidents of *The Tempest* would provide a fairly representative anthology of Elizabethan narrative invention.

Folk traditions are also represented: dressing in borrowed finery, log-bearing, monsters offering gifts, reapers and water nymphs dancing, punishment by madness and by ducking in filthy water, the drawing of all characters into a circle, songs of invitation and of summer, and a concluding procession, all have their counterparts in popular festivities. And when it was first performed *The Tempest* would have seemed so indebted to other plays that a resumé of its action might have been quickly dismissed as old fashioned, or merely fashionable. Stephano's attempt to kill Prospero is a comic sub-plot, comparable to Wagner's attempts to raise spirits in the wake of his master, Faustus. Caliban is a beast-man who could take part in many of the jigs, or burlesque after-pieces, with which Elizabethan performances were rounded off. Ben Jonson's preface to *The Alchemist*, published in 1612, says that 'the concupiscence of dances and antics so reigneth' in plays as to 'run away from nature, and be afraid of her'. But if Jonson might have complained that *The Tempest* 'tickled' the eyes of spectators in too familiar a way, another Jacobean critic acquainted with the popular improvisational comic troupes of Italy—the *Commedia dell'Arte* companies—might have suspected, as several modern scholars have done, that Shakespeare had followed the scenario or plot-outline of one of their entertainments.

But for all the parallels, analogues and echoes that have been found in earlier literature and drama, no one source has been securely identified for *The Tempest* as for other plays. Shakespeare seems to have drawn this plot from his memory, not from printed books. As far as modern scholarship can tell, it is both traditional and original.

But he did not close his mind to the influence of books. While not following a single narrative source, he did draw on other writers. The actions and words of his central character, Prospero, have been annotated from books about daemons, spirits, witches and Neo-Platonic thought: Plotinus, Bruno, St. Augustine, Cornelius Agrippa, James I (who wrote a book on *Daemonology*), and many other authorities are all relevant. The address to elves and 'demi-puppets' at the beginning of Act V is indebted to Book vii of Ovid's *Metamorphoses*, which Shakespeare seems to have known in the original Latin as well as in Golding's translation. Some scholars believe that Ferdinand's response to Miranda, the banquet and Ariel's disguise as a Harpy at the end of Act III, and Ceres' address to Juno in the Masque, are all indebted to Books i and iv of the *Aeneid*. Gonzalo's account of what he would do if he were king of the island on which he has been wrecked, is certainly indebted to 'Of Cannibals' in Florio's translation of Montaigne's *Essays;* and some hints about Caliban may have come from here. Spenser's *Faerie Queene, The Golden Legend,* various court masques, Sidney's *Arcadia* and the Bible may all be quoted to explain the implications or meaning of Shakespeare's words. The notes of modern editors furnish many examples, but one simple and one complex reference can give some impression of the ideas that are alive in *The Tempest*. In the Epilogue, where customarily the principal actor comes out of his role to ask for applause, Prospero speaks of prayer and then concludes with a simple allusion to the Lord's Prayer:

> As you from crimes would pardon'd be,
> Let your indulgence set me free.

Riddling references to many moral books and much courtly literature, however, seem to be concealed in the deceptively simple words with which Prospero decides that he will not exact revenge upon his enemies:

> . . . the rarer action is
> In virtue than in vengeance. (V. i. 27–8)

The puzzling and reverberating word is 'virtue'. 'Mercy' or 'forgiveness' would have been sufficient here; but, in avoiding these, Shakespeare has awoken further ideas of magnanimity, nobility and *'virtu'*, and of essence and purity. Many authors have been quoted in exposition: the editor of the new Arden edition uses Machiavelli, Chapman, Pico della Mirandola and the Sermon on the Mount. Jonson's masque, *Oberon, the Fairy Prince*, performed in the Banqueting House at Whitehall on New Year's Day 1611, and honouring Prince Henry, heir to the throne, also illustrates the complicated significance of the word 'virtue':

> . . . this indeed is he,
> My boys, whom you must quake at, when you see.
> He is above your reach, and neither doth
> Nor can he think within a Satyr's tooth;
> Before his presence you must fall or fly.
> He is the matter of virtue, and plac'd high.
> His meditations, to his height, are even,
> And all their issue is akin to heaven.
> He is a god, o'er kings; yet stoops he then
> Nearest a man when he doth govern men,
> To teach them by the sweetness of his sway,
> And not by force. (ll. 266–77)

One group of ideas—those concerning the discovery of the New World across the Atlantic—is reflected in the choice of an unnamed island for the setting of the play's action as well as in words and stage-business, and obviously was a comparatively new interest for Shakespeare at this time. Three reports seem to have been specially important: Sylvester Jourdain's *Discovery of the Bermudas* (1610), the Council of Virginia's *True Declaration of the State of the Colony in Virginia* (1610) and a letter by William Strachey dated July 15, 1610, and circulated in manuscript that autumn (it was published in 1625). Shakespeare's use of these news reports is pervasive and very independent. Strachey told how 'there was not a passenger, gentleman or other ... but was able to relieve his fellow and make good his course', but in *The Tempest* the ship's passengers only 'mar' the mariners' labour and 'assist the storm'. In real life, the Governor heartened every man by his 'speech and authority', but in the play the lords fall out with each other and only the Bosun, not the ship's master, has obvious authority. Like many of his contemporaries, Shakespeare read widely in the various literature about the New World; and he probably learnt much from conversation, for his friends, the Earls of Southampton and Pembroke and Sir Dudley Digges, were directly involved in the Virginia adventure. America was at once a fabled golden world, and the source of prudential, adventurous and, also, disenchanted stories. In a report from Virginia published in 1612, John Smith told how natives with grotesquely painted and decorated bodies sung and danced before him and with 'hellish cries and shouts' offered gifts of food, and tormented him by 'crowding and pressing and hanging upon him, most tediously crying, "Love you not me?".' Such events, coloured by gossip and speculative interests, are reflected in the 'strange' dances, salutations and gifts of food which greet Alonso and his courtiers. Caliban, in claiming kingship of the island and seeking for love or servitude, is like many of the natives in these reports. When Ceres gives her blessing, in the masque with which Prospero celebrates the betrothal of Ferdinand and Miranda:

> Spring come to you at the farthest,
> In the very end of harvest! (IV. i. 114–15)

she promises little more than Michael Drayton's Ode 'To the Virginia Voyage' (1606) foresaw as the fortune of the colonists:

> And cheerfully at sea
> Success you still entice,
> To get the pearl and gold
>   And ours to hold,

Virginia,
Earth's only Paradise,

Where nature hath in store
Fowl, venison, and fish,
    And the fruitful'st soil
    Without your toil
Three harvests more,
All greater than your wish. . . .

But in Shakespeare's play the promise is shown to be insubstantial; not nature, but 'So rare a wond'red father and a wise' transforms this place into a 'Paradise' (IV. i. 123–4) and, then, not in fact, but only in the enactment of his 'fancies' (ll. 121–2); it is a 'vanity of his art' (l. 41). The same island is also said to be full of 'torment, trouble, wonder and amazement': a 'fearful country' (V. i. 104–6). In the Epilogue the 'wise' father calls it a 'bare island', and considers it a prison.

Without following any one source, Shakespeare has created a play that reflects cultural and social realities of his time with alert and fascinating independence of mind.

(ii) Characters

In creating the *dramatis personae* of *The Tempest*, Shakespeare recreated a number of characters that had lived in his imagination for many years, and reformed them. For some the ancestry is plain. Gonzalo, for example, is the talkative politician, who uses laughter for his own purposes, like Menenius in *Coriolanus* or the earlier Polonius. In both his compliance with Antonio's usurpation of Prospero and his habitual honesty, he descends from the Duke of York in *Richard II* and, perhaps, Antigonus in *The Winter's Tale*. But Gonzalo's silent tears in Act V, his incredulity and his pious, humble and comprehensive sentiments, are new: he is softer, wiser and more helpless than his predecessors.

The butler and jester (the bullying fool and the weak fool; the man who does not know he is a fool and the one who does); the heir to a throne and the only daughter; the treacherous brother and the weak, resentful brother; the guilty king, the shallow courtier, and the goddesses: all these are familiar characters in Shakespeare's plays.

Yet here they are all changed: the prince woos without political considerations; the daughter's innocence is nourished by solitude; the guilty king becomes helplessly frantic; the goddesses are not real, but spirits, and 'to a strange, hollow, and confused noise, they heavily vanish'. Antonio, the treacherous brother, speaks both a compact echo of Macbeth's guilty urgency, as in:

> And by that destiny, to perform an act
> Whereof what's past is prologue, what to come
> In yours and my discharge. (II. i. 243–5)

and finishes his role with a cheap and inconsequential joke.

Ariel and Caliban are the most unexpected creations. As servants of Prospero, Ariel is more necessary than Puck to Oberon, the King of Fairies in *A Midsummer Night's Dream*, and Caliban more closely and unequivocally tied than the rebellious subjects of the early history plays to their kings, or Cloten to the King in *Cymbeline*. Ariel's intelligence is both close to Prospero's ('Thy thoughts I cleave to', IV. i. 165) and rebellious, grudging and moody. Caliban sees his plan for murderous revenge as justified by deep wrongs, by dispossession from his kingdom and subsequent slavery; in this, he is like Shylock but he outdoes this predecessor in his sensitivity to beauty and willingness to kiss the foot of a rival king, Stephano, when he offers the means for murderous revenge. At the end, Ariel is freed, and Caliban, achieving fear, wonder and a desire for 'grace', is curtly dismissed about his business.

Prospero's ancestry is most complicated. As a duke 'neglecting worldly ends' and then striving in disguise to observe other men and bring them to their better senses, he is like the Duke in *Measure for Measure*: but his powers are much greater and he manages the final confrontation with a less self-confident sense of drama. Throughout the play he cannot escape from direct responsibility to his present subjects, Ariel and Caliban, and his daughter, Miranda. As magician he descends from Oberon, and Cerimon in *Pericles*; as father from Pericles, Leontes in *The Winter's Tale*, and possibly from Leonato in *Much Ado*. As banished Duke, exchanging court life for a petty pastoral kingdom, Prospero echoes the Duke in *As You Like It*; but he is 'preserved' by his daughter not by banished lords. He is also a lonely and reflective man, concerned with 'accident', 'fortune' and 'enemies' (I. ii. 178–84); and he becomes 'distempered' by anger and fury, and acts as 'minister' of Fate. But, as a revenger, he is not like Hamlet and Lear before him; he lives to tell his own 'story', and to his enemies whom he invites to his 'poor cell'.

The spectacles, dramatic confrontations, all the longer soliloquies and speeches, the excitements and conclusion of the play, all depend on Prospero. He is on stage continuously throughout the last two Acts. No other Shakespearian character knows so much or is given so many resources; none is so continuously involved with spiritual beings. At times he seems remote from ordinary experience, yet he also speaks and acts with absolute, and immediately affecting, simplicity.

(iii) Settings

THE ISLAND

Today we think of the countryside as a natural place for poets; but in Shakespeare's day the court—the political, social, administrative, fashionable, cultural and even ecclesiastical centre of the nation—was, ideally, the poet's home. Petrarch had claimed that poets were the peers of princes; Spenser dedicated *The Faerie Queene* to Elizabeth I and prefaced it with verses addressed to various noblemen of her court. No matter how popular Shakespeare's plays became, he too could dream of

> princes to act
> And monarchs to behold the swelling scene.
> (*Henry V*, Prol.)

When he pictured the countryside, a court was not far from his mind: *Love's Labour's Lost*, *A Midsummer Night's Dream*, *As You Like It*, *The Winter's Tale* and *Cymbeline*, all relate country pleasures and pursuits to a life of sophistication and power. For *The Tempest*, set on a remote island, he avoided, for the first time, a direct representation of court life, but this decision was not made in order to escape from political and social concerns. Indeed, the play is as full as the early histories of rulers and would-be rulers, viceroys, courtiers and retainers: Sebastian, Ferdinand and Caliban claim kingship; and Ariel, Caliban, Antonio, Ferdinand and, lastly, Prospero himself look for freedom from bondage. Shakespeare is still following the renaissance vogue for pastoral poems, romances and plays that were written in and for the courts of Europe, and shares their courtly concerns together with their longing for a golden, carefree, imagined country, full of youth, music and beauty:

> Such sights as youthful poets dream
> On summer eves by haunted stream.

Gonzalo's description of a new commonwealth on the island, Ferdinand's desire to 'live here ever' (IV. i. 122), the drunken expansiveness of 'King Stephano', and Caliban's compulsive curses and dream of heavenly riches, are all Shakespeare's way of using the island to show man's political appetites extended beyond the range and scale of actual political behaviour.

A pastoral setting gave imaginative freedom. There are hints in this play of the English countryside, of hedgerows, streams and flowers, of 'green sour ringlets . . . whereof the ewe not bites', and such evocations of real sights and sounds familiarises the romantic fiction, lightens and irradiates the fancied scene. Prospero's magic, too, is helped by the setting: Robin Goodfellow, fairies and elves were familiar fictions, and in pastoral romances, like *The Faerie Queene* or *Arcadia*, invention had full scope: a clearing in the forest might reveal a fountain of cool water, with a princess combing her hair; in dark thickets were wild beasts, 'salvage men', a cave of despair; there were strange castles, hermits, holywells and enchantments; often in *The Faerie Queene* a turning in a pathway would lead to the yellow sands of a sea shore. The pastoral setting heightened danger and delight without preventing the mirroring of real and important concerns, indeed allowing this reflection a greater variety, ease and clarity.

One element in Shakespeare's customary use of pastoral settings is of particular importance in *The Tempest*. An early example is in *Titus Andronicus* where a single woodland is described by Tamora in two quite different ways. To Aaron, who is to be her lover, she exclaims:

> wherefore look'st thou sad
> When everything doth make a gleeful boast?
> The birds chant melody on every bush;
> The snakes lie rolled in the cheerful sun;
> The green leaves quiver with the cooling wind,
> And make a chequer'd shadow on the ground; . . .

But, eighty lines later, when she has been threatened, quite justly, by
Bassianus, the wood has become loathsome to her:

> A barren detested vale you see it is:
> The trees, though summer, yet forlorn and lean
> Overcome with moss and baleful mistletoe;
> Here never shines the sun; here nothing breeds,
> Unless the nightly owl or fatal raven . . .
>
> (II. iii. 10–115)

Yet a forest can bring its own peace: Valentine, in *The Two Gentlemen*,
at first believes:

> Except I be by Silvia in the night
> There is no music in the nightingale . . .

but, habituated to pastoral life, he becomes secure in thought and fancy:

> This shadowy desert, unfrequented woods,
> I better brook than flourishing peopled towns.
> Here can I sit alone, unseen of any,
> And to the nightingale's complaining notes
> Tune my distresses and record my woes.
>
> (III. i. 178–9 and V. iv. 2–6)

For Orlando, coming as a refugee to the forest in *As You Like It*, there
is a 'bleak air' in an 'uncouth' desert, where a savage prey might give
some hope of food; but stumbling into the Duke's company, with
'Forbear, and eat no more', he meets generosity and comfort, and then
we hear no more of fear or hardship. One may be weary on entering
Arden, or with hate in one's heart be in danger from lioness or snake;
but sympathising with a shepherd's passion, there is no more danger,
the beauty of the place is one's own, hatred turns to love, and here one
could 'willingly waste the time'. The beauty of the countryside is in the
heart of the beholder.

In *The Tempest*, Ferdinand scarcely notices his surroundings; he is full
of Miranda. The court party is divided and it is impossible to know who
describes it rightly: Gonzalo, who would welcome 'an acre of barren
ground, long heath, broom, furze, anything' (I. i. 62–3), and who sees
'everything advantageous to life';—or Antonio, who thinks the island is
'perfum'd by a fen' and without the 'means to live'. For Prospero,

natural beauty is always associated with his magic; he creates a masque of harvest blessings, ordered and eloquent as well as beautiful. He also knows and uses nature's harshness, threatening Ariel with being pegged in the 'knotty entrails' of an oak and Ferdinand with food of 'wither'd roots and husks'. Ariel, the spirit without human feelings, is the only one who sings clear and constantly of the island's beauties: of the yellow sands, wild waves and strange sea-beauties; and, finally and joyfully, making the island sound more like the English countryside than ever before in the play, of the cowslip and the merry summer when blossom hangs on the bough.

Shakespeare did not depict the island carelessly or indulgently: setting, character and action are closely and significantly related.

THE SEA

For Shakespeare the sea was a potent and variable image. It reminded him of war: for a battle was

> like a mighty sea
> Forc'd by the tide to combat with the wind;
> Now sways it that way, like the selfsame sea
> Forced to retire by fury of the wind . . .
> Both tugging to be victors, breast to breast,
> Yet neither conqueror nor conquered . . .
> (*3 Henry VI*, II. v. 5–12)

It could suggest overwhelming destruction and sterility:

> I stand as one upon a rock,
> Environ'd with a wilderness of sea, . . .
> Expecting ever when some envious surge
> Will in his brinish bowels swallow him.
> (*Titus*, III. i. 93–7)

A storm could be an image of chaos, the negation of all that was certain in life:

> The chidden billow seems to pelt the clouds;
> The wind-shak'd surge, with high and monstrous mane,

Seems to cast water on the burning Bear,
And quench the guards of th' ever-fixed pole.
                                    (*Othello*, II. i. 12–15)

In many plays the inconstant sea separated father from child, brother
from sister; it represented a cruel chance, so that in lonely grief Marina
thought:

This world to me is like a lasting storm,
Whirring me from my friends.
                                    (*Pericles*, IV. i. 20–1)

The sea also represented the anger and judgement of the gods; so Pericles,
shipwrecked, prays:

Yet cease your ire, you angry stars of heaven!
Wind, rain, and thunder, remember earthly man
Is but a substance that must yield to you. . . .
                                    (*Pericles*, II. i. 1ff.)

The mariner in *The Winter's Tale* thinks of more than his seamanship:

. . . the skies look grimly
And threaten present blusters. In my conscience,
The heavens with that we have in hand are angry
And frown upon 's. (III. iii. 3–6)

All these associations are awakened by the sea in *The Tempest*:
Miranda expects chaos and suffering to follow from the storm; Ariel
specifically saw 'Jove's lightnings', making even Neptune's 'bold waves
tremble'. Ferdinand, impulsively, leaps from the ship, crying 'Hell is
empty, And all the devils are here'. The King falls to his prayers;
Antonio curses the Bosun, for 'We are merely cheated of our lives by
drunkards'; Stephano finds comfort in liquor and a song; Trinculo tries
to take shelter.

The short first scene flashes a vivid and revealing light on all the
characters. In Jacobean days the point could hardly be missed. Thomas
Nashe wrote:

I cannot be persuaded any poor man, or man in misery, . . . is an
Atheist. Misery (mauger their hearts) will make them confess God.
Who heareth the thunder, that thinks not of God. . . . The black

swutty visage of the storm ... ascertains every guilty soul there is a sin-hating God. ... Why doth not the sea swallow up the earth (when as it over-peers it, and is greater than it), but that there is a God that snaffles and curbs it?

THE SUPERNATURAL

By repeating the sound-effect of thunder, Shakespeare keeps the sea-storm echoing throughout the play and makes it serve as a continuing reminder of Prospero's supernatural powers. King Alonso and the conspirators are first dismissed from the scene, and Caliban makes his first solo entry to be joined by Trinculo and Stephano, to repeated thunder. Ariel appears, disguised as a harpy, to confront the 'three men of sin' with the accompaniment of '*Thunder and lightning*'; and after this Alonso acknowledges that the heavens are angry in words that recreate the storm at sea:

> O, it is monstrous, monstrous!
> Methought the billows spoke, and told me of it;
> The winds did sing it to me; and the thunder,
> That deep and dreadful organ-pipe, pronounc'd
> The name of Prosper ... (III. iii. 95ff.)

When the masque breaks up, the accompanying '*strange, hollow and confused noise*' may again echo the storm.

But if the storm at sea was an accepted and customary representation of supernatural influences on man's life, there was nothing facile in Shakespeare's use of it. At the beginning of the second scene, before the audience can have forgotten its sound and fury, Miranda challenges the customary notions of God's justice:

> Had I been any god of power, I would
> Have sunk the sea within the earth or ere
> It should the good ship so have swallow'd and
> The fraughting souls within her. (I. ii. 10–14)

And immediately afterwards Prospero acknowledges that he, and not a god, has created the 'direful spectacle of the wreck'. In *Measure for*

Measure, Shakespeare had considered what man would do with such a power:

> Could great men thunder
> As Jove himself does, Jove would never be quiet,
> For every pelting petty officer
> Would use his heaven for thunder,
> Nothing but thunder. (II. ii. 110–14)

In the same play, the Duke in disguise as a friar watches the people he should rule and soliloquises:

> He who the sword of heaven will bear
> Should be as holy as severe; . . .
> More nor less to others paying
> Than by self-offences weighing. (III. ii. 243–8)

Before releasing his enemies from the spells he has cast upon them, Prospero claims that:

> To the dread rattling thunder
> Have I given fire, and rifted Jove's stout oak
> With his own bolt; . . . (V. i. 44–6)

Here Shakespeare pictures his hero as a man of godlike power, who could rival Jove's anger if he wished.

All the supernatural elements of the play are centred in Prospero. This is visually evident in his 'magic robes' and staff, and in his ability to watch the various enchantments, standing aloft and '*invisible*' (III. i. 15 and III. iii. 17). When the minor spirits hold the stage they are in the charge of Ariel who is tied to Prospero's will, and 'cleaves' to his thoughts. The scenes in which Prospero insists on his chief spirit's obedience, or praises his diligence, serve to make manifest through more conventional theatrical means that Prospero alone is responsible.

Shakespeare has set himself the task of creating supernatural events and also making them the result of human decision and activity. His theatrical cunning in ensuring these two, seemingly contradictory, impressions seems endlessly resourceful. For example, while using accoutrements and trick devices, he has kept Prospero's magic books off-stage and so reserved some sense of mystery about the final source of his power. Having exploited strange shapes and sounds, sudden spells, spirits enacting goddesses or nymphs and reapers, he at last uses actual garments as a trap for Stephano and Trinculo and then unleashes spirits like hounds, named Silver, Tyrant, Fury and Mountain, and urges them on as in a realistic hunt. The theatre can make almost any device work as an enchantment, but for a short time and usually once only; Shakespeare has countered this lack of sustained effectiveness by abundant invention.

And beside the basic devices of an awe-inspiring storm at sea and the magic appropriate to the English folk tradition, he makes varied use of music and dance to hold attention. When Ariel is dressed as a nymph of the sea, his boy-actor's asexual voice is given a song of enticement—'Come unto these yellow sands'—that has a chorus of rousing watch-dogs and a cock-cry. His song on the death of Alonso that follows is accompanied by a knell rung with off-stage bells or bell-like cries. Elsewhere music is used for an alarm, for a comic will-o'-the-wisp chase, and for the elaborate dance-presentations of banquet and masque. Perhaps the most affecting of all is the 'solemn air' conjured, as if from the air, by Prospero: while it sounds, his enemies, with frantic gestures, enter for the last scene and stand, silent and spell-stopped in a circle. Only Prospero comments, but the others respond without resistance:

> And as the morning steals upon the night,
> Melting the darkness, so their rising senses
> Begin to chase the ignorant fumes that mantle
> Their clearer reason. (V. i. 65–8)

It is in contrast to this 'best comforter' and 'heavenly music', that Ariel sings most merrily as he removes his master's magic robes and attires him as the Duke of Milan. Then in silence Prospero's enemies speak to him, one after another, acknowledging the man rather than the magician. There is no further music; only the almost silent obedience of Ariel as he brings other voyagers into the presence. The quiet and order of the end, after the elaborate and often noisy enchantments, speak as much for the supernatural as the thunder itself. The conclusion presents an imperfect resolution of the play's action, but the silence (or, perhaps, sadness) after music may still imply the possibility of a supernatural and harmonious existence.

(iv) Form

THE UNITIES

In *The Tempest*, Shakespeare nearly, but not quite, followed neo-classical advice to set a drama in one place and to represent not more than twenty-four hours and a single action. The change from *The Winter's Tale*, written immediately before this, which includes two countries and allows a child to be born, grow up and become betrothed, is so extreme that it should not surprise us that Shakespeare followed the rules with energy and liberty.

The first scene, at sea, breaks the restriction to an island setting once and for all, but to continuing purpose. As we have seen, the sound of the storm at sea, reverberates throughout the play. The shipwreck is alive, too, in the later dialogue, as in the newly-invented words 'sea-change', 'sea-sorrow' and 'sea-swallowed', and it is shown to be alive in the thoughts of the characters, not least in thoughts so deeply felt that they are only occasionally expressed in words:

> *Ferdinand:* Though the seas threaten, they are merciful;
>   I have curs'd them without cause. (V. i. 178-9)

> *Prospero:*   I'll deliver all;
>   And promise you calm seas, auspicious gales ... (V. i. 313-14)

Even in the Epilogue the shipwreck-scene echoes in the minds of the audience and speaker, as Prospero asks for applause (that might be thunderous):

> Gentle breath of yours my sails
> Must fill, or else my project fails,
> Which was to please.

The play is called 'The Tempest' and it is arguable that its first, oddly located scene is the fullest representation of one of its basic themes, the turbulence (and necessary control) of nature, life and imagination. The other island scenes float, as it were, upon its concentrated evocation of chaos, power and human helplessness.

In restricting the time of the play's action, Shakespeare cut down from the regulation twenty-four hours to about four. The ways in which he achieved this have wide repercussions on the effect of the performance. Firstly he used the customary device of reporting past events in the dialogue, but he made Prospero, his hero, almost the only mouthpiece; the second scene is largely a recounting of events by him or at his instigation, and he remains on stage continuously. As for the events shown in action, the odd thing is that they could have taken almost any length of time; indeed a week, a month or, even, a year, would seem to be more proper for the hatching of two rebellions, and the separate trial, punishment and re-acceptance of almost all the characters. But Shakespeare makes Prospero force the pace and, again, act as sole agent in this. On several occasions he asks Ariel the time of the day, even when he seems to know the answer himself (I. ii. 239–40). He requires 'diligence' and 'quick motion', and from early in his first scene, he is aware of the demands of 'the very minute' (l. 37). Prospero is the chief means whereby the audience is made aware of the past and present; and in his last speech to Alonso he looks ahead to the following night, that will pass 'quick away', and then beyond that to the gap of time until his own death. By conforming his action to a rigorous time-scheme, Shakespeare has not been concerned with probability or a straight-forward kind of dramatic illusion; he has shown Prospero creating—or 'courting' (I. ii. 183)—a crisis of fortune. Indeed Prospero arranges action and speaks of time as if he were a dramatist seeking a concentrated and meaningful intensity, an energetic dream-like awareness; but he does so in order to take part in the crisis himself, for his own far-reaching purposes.

The unity of theme is still less simple. On the one hand, action all stems from Prospero; he is almost like the witty servant of a classical comedy, turned master and become serious, and taking a single opportunity that has come to him. But on the other hand, the various characters whom Prospero controls work for their own ends, without knowledge or comprehension of his means or purposes. Ariel, his most sensitive spirit, 'cleaves' to Prospero's thoughts (IV. i. 165), but only under duress; given his freedom, he parts without word of thanks or feeling. His daughter, whose infant smile had sustained him when he first came to the island, now breaks and forgets his commands; and when he is 'touched with anger' more than ever before (IV. i. 144–5), she takes dismissal without demur, being powerless to help. Caliban was first loved and then rigorously punished for his misdeeds, yet he can still see the drunken Stephano as a fit rival to his old master; when at last he recognises the difference, Prospero at once dismisses him about household chores. The characters from the wreck have their own concerns and, with the exception of Ferdinand, do not meet Prospero until the last scene of all. He controls their fortunes and actions, and even their moral awareness, but desires and reactions are their own, right through the play. Prospero is affected by the feelings of others, especially his daughter's happiness, Gonzalo's tears, and Alonso's grief for the loss of his son, and by the responses of Caliban and Ariel; but the theme of the play, in so far as it is the 'story of his life', will 'take the ear strangely', however much the others 'long to hear' it (V. i. 304–14). The action of the play is unified without loss of diversity, both of incident and intention, and without rendering comprehension either simple or certain.

NARRATIVE

The unfolding of the four-hour narrative is managed so that each strand has its own distinctive presentation. Prospero has soliloquies, asides and sustained speeches to accentuate his private thoughts as distinct from those he can share with others. As soon as he has set the action afoot in Act I, he appears in the next two Acts only invisibly; but he returns to full intervention in the final two Acts, continually dominating and in both having solo moments, in the first to call Ariel and in the last to abjure his 'rough magic'.

The politicians from Milan and Naples are introduced together, talking on diverse topics, but with Alonso as an almost silent centre. For the rest of the play, until the last scene, they are engaged in a determined search to find Ferdinand and for an opportunity for Antonio to kill Alonso, and then in a desperate and frenzied search for suicide or fresh horror. In contrast, Caliban, Trinculo and Stephano are brought together with three prolonged solo entries, but this and their next scene, that very soon follows, both end with a comic procession to search for and destroy Prospero. In their third scene, they are deflected from their purpose by their interest in gaudy regal clothes, and are then sent off roaring in ignominious flight. These two strands, both full of resentment, conspiracy, and pursuit are interwoven so that their episodes can be seen comparatively, the one often defining the other.

The third strand subsidiary to Prospero's, concerns Ferdinand, his grief for the loss of his father and his courtship of Miranda. The lovers meet at the end of Prospero's first scene and under his control, but after the two conspiracy narratives have been established, they meet, as they think, alone. Ferdinand has a soliloquy now, but when Miranda enters Prospero is '*at a distance, unseen*'; the quietest scene in the whole play, with concern, delight, tears and silent joy, ends quickly, for as soon as they have plighted hearts they run away and Prospero remains for soliloquy; there seems something dangerous, uncontainable, even here. When father, daughter and son-in-law to be, meet at the beginning of Act IV, the action again seems to stand still, this time for the ceremony of betrothal and its celebratory masque. Yet as this reaches its fullest development, there is a sudden and quite unexpected development when Prospero '*suddenly starts*', destroys the masque, asks them to bear with his 'weakness', and dismisses them. Here the Caliban–Stephano narrative comes back to attention:

> I had forgot that foul conspiracy
> Of the beast Caliban and his confederates
> Against my life. (IV. i. 139–41)

The relation between these two strands had earlier been stated by a grotesque visual comparison when Ferdinand entered bearing a log— perhaps the very same one—as Caliban had done, both being compelled to do Prospero's bidding. Before the masque and, by implication, within it, Prospero had warned Ferdinand against the 'fire' in his blood and against 'wanton charms', and so here again this young prince is related to Caliban who earlier had sought to 'violate the honour' of Miranda and now promises her to Stephano.

The concluding scene, for the first and last time, draws all strands together including the doings of the Master and Bosun from Act I, scene i. It is controlled precisely by Prospero, who dressed as the Duke of Milan brings each character face to face with each other and with himself. Now, however, there are no spirits at all, except Ariel visible and audible to Prospero alone. The movement off stage at the end is eloquently unremarkable: the earlier processions, chases, and various manifestations of bondage, are here summed up in this *exeunt* with no music and no verbal response to the concluding words 'Please you, draw near.' In similar ways to this, each incident of the multiple narrative gains meaning and effect by the reflection of other, analogous incidents.

REVELS

The betrothal masque in Act IV may be considered as a play-within-the-play, giving a timeless and general representation of the Ferdinand and Miranda narrative and illustrating the elaborate power of Prospero's art. But its importance is greater than this. Firstly, whatever delight Ferdinand and the theatre audience take in its performance, to Prospero it is at first but 'some vanity of mine art', exercised for the 'young couple' (IV. i. 40–2). Secondly, it contains the announcement that Cupid has 'broke his arrows' and 'Swears he will shoot no more'. This message is probably forgotten as Juno and Ceres join to bless the young couple, but as the nymphs and sicklemen draw near the end of their *'graceful dance'*, Prospero *'starts suddenly, and speaks'* (l. 138, S.D.). Now the masque-master, who is enacting his 'present fancies', breaks up the masque in a strong 'passion' (ll. 143–4): 'Well done; avoid; no more!' The imagination which created the masque also destroys it.

The *'strange, hollow, and confused noise'* with which the spirits *'heavily vanish'*, we have already considered as an echo of the tempest that starts the play. This is not merely an aural echo, for the masque should be seen as one in a series of elaborate stage spectacles or 'revels' as they might be called by a Jacobean used to court entertainments. The whole shape of the play in performance depends largely on the placing of these elements, all involving a large number of supernumerary actors or dancers and accompanied by music or noise, and all in effective contrast with the longer scenes of dialogue when usually not more than four or five speakers are involved at any one time.

The first scene is the first of the revels. On the printed page it looks like a sequence of broken dialogue, but once the actors are on stage in rehearsal it is clearly a corporate and physical effect. The activity required by the words—the 'bestirring', pulling on ropes, marring of labour; the praying, ordering, cursing and 'howling'—suggests abundant life and it is given the varied accompaniment of wind, whistle, thunder, lightning and, finally, the sound of the ship splitting. The whole scene has to be carefully ordered, or choreographed, if the words are to be heard or the action to become sufficiently clear. Whether realistically or simply staged, the stage-picture will be elaborate and varied, moving towards a thunderous climax after which Gonzalo's desperate bargaining for life is heard. The next scene starts with a composed and silent Prospero and an urgent Miranda, a striking contrast: the voice of a young girl the only apparent echo to the earlier storm.

Act II has no full revels scene, but it concludes with Stephano, and Trinculo joining Caliban in a drunken song (and probably dance) of freedom. Act III, however, concludes with the presentation of the banquet in masque-like dance and music. This is not unbounded chaos but a temptation, subtle and complicated:

> Solemn and strange music; and Prospero on the top, invisible. Enter several strange shapes, bringing in a banquet; and dance about it with gentle actions of salutations; and inviting the King, etc., to eat, they depart.

The dialogue makes the intended effect a little clearer: the politicians are invited to eat a banquet by 'monstrous' creatures who are physically and perhaps obscenely deformed and who obviously induce fear; yet the music is 'sweet' and their manners 'gentle'. The 'strange shapes' say nothing, so they must be interpreted; and the politicians argue, as convenience and hunger dictate, that they are 'kind', or 'natural' to the island and human life; only Alonso retains any sense of fear. Then, having made their desires their guide, the politicians 'stand to, and feed'; and at once the storm breaks:

> Thunder and lightning. Enter Ariel, like a harpy; claps his wings upon the table; and, with a quaint device, the banquet vanishes.

Ariel's disguise is purposeful: in early mythology harpies were personifications of whirlwinds and hurricanes, appropriate to a tempest; but in the *Aeneid* and later, they became filthy, loathsome and rapacious creatures with the body of a woman and the talons and head of a carrion bird; Virgil called them 'dark', and they were the instruments of divine vengeance. Prospero later says that Ariel's harpy had a 'devouring' grace (III. iii. 84).

The effect is both showy and dramatic: the monstrous-gentle creatures leave the banquet; fearful debate leads to a resolution to accept the gift; a whirlwind figure of rapacious vengeance strikes his wings, and the banquet vanishes. Judgement follows: 'You are three men of sin . . . ', and Ariel, acting on Prospero's instructions and speaking more like his master than anywhere else, convicts them of their crimes and vows lingering and desolate perdition as the only alternative to heart's sorrow and 'a clear life ensuing'. He vanishes in more thunder, and then with 'soft music' the monstrous creatures re-enter to remove the table and taunt the silent watchers with 'mocks and mows'. As after the sea tempest, Prospero is calm, but he leaves his 'enemies' in 'distractions' and 'fits', so that Gonzalo and the others expect them to take their own lives.

The betrothal and its masque follow straightaway at the beginning of Act IV, again calling for a large number of supernumerary actors and for dances. This time Prospero does not remain 'collected', and before the end of the Act there is a further crowded scene, like a revel. Now Prospero, with Ariel to help, sets the returning spirits on a wild chase. The victims, Stephano, Trinculo and Caliban, are dressed or loaded with glistening apparel, but they are swept up by the entering 'spirits, in shape of dogs and hounds.' As soon as 'a noise of hunters' is heard, their quarry is silent and then they add to the yelps and cries with their roaring. This revel scene is on one note, brutal and noisy, and augmented by its creator's cries; comic, perhaps, in so far as the responses of the pursued can be distinguished; and continuing without rebate from the moment it is unleashed until the stage is again nearly empty. Prospero then holds attention for the end of the Act, promising Ariel freedom.

The obvious conclusion to this series of revels would be a more sumptuous and fully harmonious pageant for the end of the play: adaptations of the text in Restoration England added a Masque of Neptune complete with songs and dances. And when Prospero dresses as Duke of Milan, calls for music and draws a magic circle on the ground, this expectation seems about to be satisfied: but the politicians enter frantically and are slowly released from their spells to make their highly individual responses: Shakespeare (and Prospero) has rejected the expected, group climax. The nearest approach to a concerted dramatic display is when Prospero 'discovers' (V. i. 171, S.D.) Ferdinand and Miranda playing chess, and even this is not so splendid and unified as it might be. The first words are 'Sweet lord, you play me false' and, after the lovers' loving wrangling, Miranda views the assembled men and wonders at them as a brave new world presented to her—for Miranda, they have transformed the scene, as if in a masque. The theatre audience must accept the silent *exeunt* of the individual characters as conclusion to the spectacular events of the whole play.

FIVE ACTS

At the Blackfriars Theatre, the King's Men continued a practice, that had started when this more select theatre had been used by companies of boy actors, and sometimes played music between each Act of a play. John Webster's *Duchess of Malfi* clearly depends on these four intervals for both narrative clarity and character development.[1] In *The Tempest*, one incident suggests that here Shakespeare also wrote with this custom especially in mind. At the end of Act IV Prospero and Ariel *exeunt* and for the very next line, at the beginning of the next Act, Prospero has to re-enter dressed '*in his magic robes*'. Clearly this costume-change took a little time; in Act I, scene ii, Prospero asks Miranda to help 'pluck my magic garment from me' as if it was more than he could easily manage himself, and for Act V he probably had further costume changes to prepare underneath the robes so that with the addition of the 'hat and rapier' (l. 84) that Ariel brings he will be revealed as Duke of Milan. Either there was a pause between the *exeunt* and the re-entry, or else music was played. The second is more likely, for a silence while the stage is empty needs special textual or musical preparation if it is not to seem an unwanted and inefficient hiatus. The pursuit of Caliban, Stephano and Trinculo, which has just led off stage boisterously or perhaps horribly, would indicate an appropriate style of music against which Prospero's return with 'Now does my project gather to a head' would sound with an added effect of severe control.

The Tempest is a short play by Shakespearian standards so there would be time enough for music between acts. Moreover the manner in which Acts close and open, and the difference between each Act-interval, indicate that Shakespeare was consciously exploiting this structural device.

[1] See Revels Plays edition (1964), p. xxiii and n. i.

At the end of Act I Ferdinand is charmed to silence and obedience, and leaves together with Miranda and Ariel, and with Prospero clearly in command of all three. At the start of Act II, Alonso, Ferdinand's father, enters ineffectually ordering his fractious nobles to be silent.

Act II ends with an uproarious *exeunt* for Caliban, Stephano and Trinculo, crying 'High-day Freedom!', in insurrection; Act III begins quietly with Ferdinand carrying Caliban's burden.

Act III ends with the desperation and 'ecstacy' of Alonso, Antonio and Sebastian, Prospero's power over his enemies being made evident by his soliloquy immediately before this: 'They now are in my power'. But Act IV opens with Prospero at the formal bethrothal of Ferdinand and Miranda, beginning with a new note: 'If I have too austerely punish'd you.'

Between Acts IV and V, as we have seen, Prospero's hounds, Fury, Tyrant, Mountain and Silver are at work, and Prospero prepares for the last manifestations of his magic powers; this gives dramatic tension before the abjuration of those powers.

If Shakespeare did intend these intervals to be marked clearly by music, he was using them and the general structure of the play to accentuate certain aspects of its action. Prospero's power and responsibility are thus spotlit, and likewise the bondage and freedom of both visitors and inhabitants of his island, those who come within his sphere of influence.

(v) *Style*

The dialogue of *The Tempest* is muscular and compact. The syntax often pulls against the longer paced iambic pentameters of the verseform. Images, metaphors and similes are not indulged; they are strong, sensuous and often surprising, but they are tight-reined. Occasionally speech is phrased pedantically or with severe formality; but as often it has an every-day simplicity. So in the last scene, Prospero guides Alonso towards an understanding of his true situation:

> *Alonso:*   If thou beest Prospero,
>   Give us particulars of thy preservation;
>   How thou hast met us here, whom three hours since
>   Were wreck'd upon this shore; where I have lost—

How sharp the point of this remembrance is!—
My dear son Ferdinand.
Prospero: I am woe for't, sir.
Alonso: Irreparable is the loss; and patience
Says it is past her cure.
Prospero: I rather think
You have not sought her help, of whose soft grace
For the like loss I have her sovereign aid,
And rest myself content.
Alonso: You the like loss!
Prospero: As great to me as late; and, supportable
To make the dear loss, have I means much weaker
Than you may call to comfort you, for I
Have lost my daughter.
Alonso: A daughter!
O heavens, that they were living both in Naples,
The King and Queen there! That they were, I wish
Myself were mudded in that oozy bed
Where my son lies. When did you lose your daughter?
Prospero: In this last tempest. I perceive these lords
At this encounter do so much admire
That they devour their reason, . . .

As Prospero says 'In this last tempest' in this context, he reanimates the
whole course of the play, and expresses both the storm and tranquillity
of his own consciousness. From this memory he turns simply and wholly
to the others on stage, who include his enemies. The image implicit
in 'devour', can represent the pain and avidity of their concerns; it
may also echo back to the harpy which had a 'grace . . . devouring'.

   This passage also illustrates how deep feeling is expressed with both
immediacy and concentration. The first speech of Alonso is broken with
sudden grief, represented by a parenthesis and word-play on 'point'.
Prospero's reply, with 'soft grace' and 'sovereign aid' juxtaposed and
yet held apart by the syntax, has a longer phrased strength, introduced
with 'I rather think' carefully completing the verse-line, and concluding
with a steadiness that gives weight to simple words: 'And rest myself
content'. Alonso's response is sharp, cutting back verbally to 'loss' of the
previous line and, with the initial 'You', breaking the regular iambics.
Prospero's next speech has a syntactical complexity beyond that strictly

necessary for sense or metre, representing a wary carefulness of thought and feeling. Alonso's cries are soon checked with the reflective 'That they were'; but as the syntax becomes more sustaining the imagery, in 'mudded' and 'oozy', is both surprising, physical and directly evocative, within short compass.

There are relatively few long speeches in the play: Ariel's description of the wreck and his denunciation of the 'men of sin', Gonzalo's account of an ideal commonwealth and Caliban's of his dreams, and several for Prospero—his narration of past events in Act I, his apology after the masque and then his invocation and renunciation of his spiritual powers. Prospero also speaks without interruption as his enemies come to their senses in the last scene, but this changes frequently between soliloquy, description and address to individual members of the group. Such variation is more in keeping with the style of the play as a whole which uses shorter speeches and keeps a full stage-picture alive by introducing asides or sudden changes of subject or speaker. Even the comics, Stephano and Trinculo, after their first solo entries exchange an individual presentation for much shorter and more varied interchanges than usual in such roles in Shakespeare's plays. And the comic scenes also contain Caliban, who brings to the drunken comedy additional, and unusual, ingredients: sensitive evocation of physical beauty, animal affection and conspiracy for cruel vengeance.

The style of *The Tempest* ensures that the audience's focus on the play is basically wide. There is deep feeling, crucial and exciting thought, comedy and poetic fantasy: but no one element is sustained for long, and no one character, except Prospero, dominates the picture for long. Even the central figure does not seem open to the audience, as do Hamlet, Lear, Pericles, Imogen, or Hermione, Paulina and Leontes. At the central crisis of *The Winter's Tale* when Paulina announces the death of Hermione (III. ii.), Leontes is silent; but Paulina speaks and guides the audience's consciousness of what is happening, and then Leontes speaks directly of his shame and sorrow. When he is reunited with Perdita and Hermione, his growing consciousness of new hope and love breaks slowly, delicately and strongly, in a sustained sequence of emotional and physical responses until, reunited with his Queen, he commands the end of the play. However, at the first major crisis of *The Tempest*, when the masque is stopped, the onlookers cannot understand what has happened:

Prospero settles his mind in silence—'a turn or two I'll walk to still my beating mind'—and then denounces Caliban as 'born devil'; after the collapse of the comic insurrection he sets the spirit-hounds after their quarry. There is no doubt that Prospero's reaction threatens his self-control and his purposes, but the struggle takes place at a remove: why does he remember Caliban at this moment? why is he more 'distempered' with anger than ever before in Miranda's memory? why is there no soliloquy? why tell Ferdinand that life is like a 'dream'? The audience must be, in part, perplexed.

The second major crisis, at the beginning of Act V, is a development from the first but less intense and exciting; it sounds like an outward expression of a decision already made. Some surprise is registered when Prospero realises that Ariel expects his 'affections would become tender' if he could see Gonzalo's wintery tears, but then his speech is compact and precise with accomplished decision:

> Though with their high wrongs I am struck to th' quick,
> Yet with my nobler reason 'gainst my fury
> Do I take part; the rarer action is
> In virtue than in vengeance; they being penitent,
> The sole drift of my purpose doth extend
> Not a frown further. (ll. 25–30)

In the event, his enemies are not all penitent or, rather, they are presented so that it seems they are not thoroughly so; yet Prospero does not punish any more. His moment of decision had not only come with something like inevitability, but it was also capable of fuller development. It seems almost a mystery, even this last phase of crisis, that changes Prospero from a man of power—'At this hour, Lies at my mercy all mine enemies'—to the restored Duke of the play's last moments, and then to the lonely man of the Epilogue, needing mercy and freedom from his own 'faults'.

In *The Tempest* Shakespeare has modified his style so that the audience is kept from identifying themselves consistently with any one character. Even the central figure, whose mind and actions control the whole narrative, is kept at a distance. The characters are no less fully realised than those of earlier plays—their reactions are varied, idiosyncratic, immediate, deep-seated, complex—but they do not grow into the usual

Shakespearian magnificence of individuality. The energy of Shakespeare's creative mind is tightly contained by his choice of style, his handling of the drama in words and action. More than for any other of his plays, the audience must sit back and observe the whole; they cannot be drawn into one character's distinct, and therefore limited, response to the action; —except, perhaps, to Prospero in the epilogue, but even there proverbial language and octosyllabic couplets prevent empathetic indulgence.

The wide view, that Shakespeare insists upon, is not passive. For all the obvious physical, temperamental and verbal beauty of the play, for all the smoothness of plot and counterplots and the intricate complexity of the conclusion, the most sustained impression of the play in action may be that of a tempest about to overwhelm both great and insignificant from without and from within their own beings: the turbulence at the roots of life seems to be at one with the hidden and contained energy of the dramatic writing.

3. The Image of Nature

The purpose of playing, according to Shakespeare's Hamlet, is 'as 'twere', to hold a mirror up to nature. For two principal reasons the image of *The Tempest* has become obscured in the nineteenth and twentieth centuries. Firstly the supernatural, poetic and fantastic elements have tended to prevent readers, actors and theatre directors from seeing the realistic, everyday and frightening elements. Secondly, the development of scenic, lighting and sound devices in our theatres has encouraged spectacular productions which visually remove the play from life outside the theatre.

To see nature, as we know it, within the play's mirror, a performance or reading that takes account of the unusual dramatic style, and its containment of great energy and individual drama, is the only necessity. Then form, setting, characters and ideas can spring alive, enriched by the most fanciful elaboration of the island, magic or narrative.

Of course, Prospero, Caliban, Ariel and Miranda could not walk the streets of today's world; but within the play they make tangible some of the hidden forces in our own lives and in our political, social and cultural context. Prospero is a man of great power: he has brought the dead back to existence; he could slowly and painfully kill his enemies. He can influence others by evoking huge and sensual images of horror or paradisal content. He has engineered the situation, with attendant water nymph, in which Ferdinand desires Miranda. Miranda had earlier preserved his will to survive with her smiles, and yet, for his own ends, he threatens her with hatred and tells her that Ferdinand is but a Caliban to other men (I. ii. 475–81). He can seem to ignore Caliban's final assertion that he will seek for 'grace' (V. i. 295) and threaten Ariel, whose nature it is to be free as air and fire, with twelve winters 'pegged' within the knotty entrails of an oak (I. ii. 295). He has, in short, power which is analogous to that modern power which we all acknowledge but find hard to imagine in actual and responsible terms: his hand might be on a button that could explode atom bombs or set in motion the resistless persuasion of the electronic media of communication. To represent such a man in a theatre, fancy is often more potent, more familiar and recognisable than fact or simple fiction.

Prospero is a self-consciously wise man; he has studied for the better-ment of his mind and prides himself on the recognition of both good and ill affections in others. Yet at the climax of the play his 'nobler reason' is threatened, and almost overcome, by his 'fury' (V. i. 26). For Shakespeare 'fury' was a madness, a bestial, uncontrollable, destructive anger:[1] and he shows this unleashed within Prospero at the height of the betrothal masque, when the nymphs, representing air and water, and the sicklemen, representing fire and earth, are about to reach the close of their dance 'encounter'. This image of harmony and accord provides the most dangerous moment for Prospero. The spirits have done 'well' in presenting his 'present fancies' but he cannot follow wholly: he remembers 'the beast Caliban and his confederates'; life seems like an insubstantial pageant; he feels the need to comfort Ferdinand and Miranda. So he says that life melts, dissolves and fades, and he also says it is like their present revels which '*to a strange, hollow and confused noise . . . heavily*' vanished. Of himself he says, only, that he is 'vexed' and 'troubled', but truly he is angry and defeated:

> A devil, a born devil, on whose nature
> Nurture can never stick; on whom my pains,
> Humanely taken, all, all lost, quite lost;
> And as with age his body uglier grows,
> So his mind cankers. (IV. i. 188–92)

Caliban, son of a witch, is his obvious failure and Prospero, at his most idealistic, imaginative and hopeful, cannot forget him; this element of human life cannot be ignored, for it has its individual energy within his own mind as without it. Caliban is no real threat to Prospero's life as Ariel makes clear (see III. ii. 59 and 111 and IV. i. 170–84); but Prospero cannot eliminate him. He is helpless in this, and can only escalate pain:

> I will plague them all,
> Even to roaring. (ll. 192–3)

[1] Compare, for example, *Com. Err.*, IV. ii. 35; *Much Ado*, I. i. 163; *Tam. Shr.*, II. i. 132; *I Hen. VI*, IV. iii. 28; *Rom. & Jul.*, III. iii. 111; *Timon*, III. v. 70; *Macb.*, V. ii. 14; *Lear*, III. i. 9; and III. iv. 128; *Ant. & Cl.*, II. v. 40.

His imaginative, quick, sensitive spirit, Ariel, is summoned only to trap the foolish confederates and then to plague them.

This crisis of power and conscience passes into the last scene with its choice of 'virtue' not 'vengeance', and then its compromises, forbearance and purposeful reassumption of responsibility and social life. Two of the most acutely realised moments of this group conclusion are when Prospero sees that his enemies are a 'brave new world' to Miranda —he comments with understanding and wide awareness, ' 'Tis new to thee'—and when Prospero acknowledges Caliban:

> this thing of darkness I
> Acknowledge mine, (ll. 275–6)

and Caliban answers by expecting only more punishment 'I shall be pinch'd to death': Prospero can neither protect Miranda from disappointment nor discover himself to Caliban in other than a fearful and repressive manner. A third sharply felt moment, and almost the very last moment of the play, is when Prospero dismisses Ariel:

> My Ariel, chick,
> That is thy charge. Then to the elements
> Be free, and fare thou well!

The agent of his power, and the spirit attentive to his quickest and most far-reaching thought, disappears without reply: there is no feed-back from Prospero's endearment or farewell.

In performance the play is unassertive, but holds the mirror up to nature for us to view wholly, steadily and intently.

4. *The Play in Performance*

The predominantly wide focus for which *The Tempest* has been written makes it more than usually necessary for the reader of the play to keep a full stage-picture in his mind's eye and to be watchful for those short moments of intense individual feeling that grow to full power only through the actors' embodiment. The following commentary is designed to be read with the text of the play open for reference beside this book.

I. i

The Master and the King of Naples take charge of mariners and politicians at first; but Alonso is already too late to find the Master, and is ordered below by the Bosun who is now in command on deck.

Entries, exits and re-entries give an increasing tempo to the scene as their phrasing becomes shorter. The mariners at first work silently, but their re-entry '*wet*' brings staccato, repetitive sound, and marks the climax by urgent prayers to the powers that are thought to show their anger through the storm. The activity moves off-stage for the cries of 'We split, we split!' and so the desperation of Antonio, Sebastian and Gonzalo is spotlit on the now empty stage; and the greater apparent size of the stage after the crowded activity will show the isolation of each man as he prepares for death.

The stage-direction requiring a '*confused noise within*' uses the same words as that at the break-up of the masque (IV. i. 138) and should have a similar quality. Against this the reactions of human beings are probably contrasted: compare Ariel's account:

> Not a soul
> But felt a fever of the mad and play'd
> Some tricks of desperation. (I. ii. 208 10)

I. ii

Prospero in his 'magic garment' (l. 24) is silent and, presumably, 'collected' (l. 13) and still. Miranda is an absolute contrast: she begins by pleading with her father but, when he does not reply immediately, she changes to various kinds of soliloquy—descriptive, ejaculatory and reflective. The audience, knowing nothing of Prospero at this stage of the play, may well think that her 'god of power' refers to the ceremonially garbed figure that remains unmoved by her obvious feeling and concern. When he does speak Miranda can only exclaim helplessly, and Prospero has to repeat 'No harm'. Intimacy between father and daughter is not fully established until the robe is laid aside and he acknowledges her tears (l. 25).

Prospero's long narration that follows is varied at first with thoughts of Miranda, so that in assuring her she is a princess he lightens the tone with a jest about her mother and finally refers to Miranda in the third person as thy father's 'only heir' (l. 58); Miranda immediately exchanges this for the first person plural, 'we', and intimacy is closest with 'my girl' that follows. But when Prospero tells of his brother he is caught up in 'dark' feelings (l. 50) and self-concern. He speaks of his own neglect of 'state' and, then, suddenly returning to 'Thy false uncle', he stops, probably involuntarily, for 'Dost thou attend me?' But he is not playing the careful pedagogue; he is greatly affected by his own narration. He returns to it with far greater energy; first a tightly phrased series of participle clauses and then, on 'mine', the reiteration of 'I say', and two corrections that sharpen the imagery and twice disturb the run of the syntax. He now speaks of himself in the more measured image of ivy destroying the tree on which it climbs, but at once the rhythm quickens again with two brusque addresses to Miranda. Now he repeats himself in much longer phrasing to give a fuller account until, on 'Hence his ambition growing', a more direct statement again awakens thought of Miranda. The next and crucial passage is sharpened and complicated by three parentheses, and by self-directed sarcasm. Prospero had said earlier that he had 'done nothing but in care' of his dear daughter, but now, clearly, he is deeply moved by his brother's treachery and his own wrongs: this is made apparent by changes of tone, tempo, focus and physical performance. His account is softened only by Miranda's more active participation (ll. 132ff.), a change which serves to dramatise his dependence on her affection. The scene now moves forward with the separate introductions of Ariel and Caliban, on whom Prospero also depends.

At this point Prospero's magic powers are also first directly dramatised, as he charms Miranda to sleep. Then Ariel enters, with alert address to a 'great' and 'grave' master. Prospero's later descriptions of 'my bird' and 'chick', and the spirit's association with fire and air, are guiding ideas for deciding what Ariel should look like. The young movements and voice of a boy actor would help to distinguish him (and the other spirits) in Jacobean performances, but in any production the enactment of the many cues for Ariel's energetic activity and speed will achieve something of the appropriate contrast. He has free thoughts, too, for he can illustrate the suffering of Ferdinand to make a joke with 'His arms in this sad knot' (l. 224).

Ariel's cry for 'My liberty' (l. 245) is eloquent in its comprehensive and contrasting brevity, and it awakens a dangerous repressive force in Prospero. If the later cue 'Thy thoughts I cleave to' (IV. i. 165) is taken to indicate that the spirit can indeed be tied to *be* what Prospero thinks, then the following incident is harsh and painful. 'Once a month' Prospero punishes Ariel by making him re-live the torments of Sycorax (ll. 261-3): hence the cowed responses of Ariel, Prospero's sarcasm (e.g. 'O, was she so?'), and the new physical quality of his language (see especially ll. 252-6, 259, 280-1, 287-9, 294-6). From a free, powerful and spritely figure, Ariel changes to a painfully distorted one, who groans and howls in realisation of past and threatened torments; he is now, to Prospero, a 'malignant thing' (l. 257) to be confined like Caliban. But on submission he is again alert and sent on business, to turn himself into a 'nymph o' th' sea'; Prospero's affectionate words to wake Miranda show that he, too, is once more relaxed and calm. Then Caliban is called, Shakespeare taking occasion for Prospero to remind Miranda and the audience that this 'slave' (l. 308) is necessary to them. Miranda is awoken expressly to see 'a villain' she does not 'love to look on'; Prospero's reason for this is not explained directly but his later comparison of Ferdinand to Caliban (l. 480) may possibly mean that he wished to provide a contrast before bringing her face to face with the man he wishes her to marry. Neither is the need for Ariel's disguise as a nymph and his seductive song (ll. 375ff.) explained: again Prospero may be trying to influence the encounter which he cannot directly control; his soul 'prompts' (l. 420), but success is dependent on the free affections and exchange of 'eyes' (l. 441) of the young people.

Before Caliban answers his summons, Ariel returns briefly in his disguise, attentive and 'quaint': the slow movements and the earthy and dark language of Caliban are the more effective by contrast. His invocation of his mother and his recollection of Prospero's earlier care and his own responsive love, all take up themes of parenthood, usurpation and concern from previous incidents in this scene; his memory of being 'mine own king' (l. 342) echoes Ariel's demand for liberty. Prospero again retaliates by narrating past events—'thou didst seek to violate the honour of my child'—but Caliban's response, unlike Ariel's, is laughter and exultation at the very thought. As Prospero controlled Ariel so he controls Caliban, promising renewed torments to make him 'roar'. Finally Caliban leaves silently, but only after an aside showing his rebellious will resisting the enforced slavery: he carries a threat with him. His entry has accomplished nothing tangible towards the progress of the play's action; instead it has demonstrated more completely the nature of Prospero's power: it has uncovered passions and tenderness, developed an impression of the natural resources of the island, brought a witch and the devil into the story, and shown, by Caliban's laughter and continued resistance, the limitations of Prospero's and Miranda's influence.

Ariel's song draws silence from Prospero and Miranda, its 'sweet air' giving peacefulness to the stage for the first time; only 'watch dogs' and 'strutting chanticleer' of the refrain continue stronger intimations. The encounter with Ferdinand is at first touched with grief and the delicate formality of Prospero's 'fringed curtains' (l. 408, etc.), but quickly it draws a warmer tone, Prospero leading in this. Ariel continues on stage and repeated praise of his achievement (see ll. 420–1, 441–2, 493 and 494–5) suggests that he continues to lead and restrain Ferdinand in the contrived meeting. (In performance this frequently gives natural scope for mischievous comedy.) But the incident also continues the earlier interests as the confrontation of Caliban had done: Prospero has to repress both Ferdinand and Miranda with promises of confinement and punishment. (In his concluding speech, Ferdinand suggests that, to the free mind, liberty may be found in bondage.) The energy of Prospero's rebukes is surprising, especially towards Miranda; it is explained only as an expression of his fear 'lest too light winning Make the prize light' (ll. 451–2). Prospero is both delighted and afraid; he keeps Ariel close at his side, as he forces the scene to a close.

Besides completing a long narration, I. ii. has established personal affections and dependence; rebellion, freedom and sovereignty; pent-up and released passions; magic control and its limitations; pain, fear and happiness.

II. i.

Alonso, as King, enters first and remains at the centre of the court-in-exile (like the banished Duke in *As You Like It*). But although he is often addressed, his own words are very few; the talk ricochets around him, often with forced and sometimes cruel humour, and once with attempted precision about a magical occurence. When Alonso speaks more than a brief phrase he is clearly a man torn by grief and self-criticism, and by fantasy: 'what strange fish Hath made his meal on thee' (ll. 106–7). The hopeful and careful speech of Francisco does not help him, and Sebastian's reproach simply feeds his self-concern.

In this strained, unnatural and frequently trivial kingdom, Gonzalo's extensive talk of a pure and innocent commonwealth without sovereignty has many repercussions. Such a 'Golden Age' is neither jest nor dream for Alonso (see l. 164); and after viewing the other kingdom of daughter, spirit and bestial creature in the previous scene, the audience may instinctively make further critical comparisons. Gonzalo's more sustained talk also helps to mark by contrast the dispersed and nervous quality of the rest of the dialogue, and it yields to renewed exchange of cheap sarcasm and recrimination. Nothing is happening, nor is likely to happen; and then Shakespeare has Ariel enter invisible with '*solemn music*' to put all but Sebastian and Antonio asleep, probably with some comic incidents (see ll. 194–5).

It is then that the slow and dispersed effect of this scene is counter-stated by active imagination (l. 199) and purposeful plotting. From 'standing water' (l. 212) Sebastian is roused by Antonio's packed, careful speeches until he sees himself 'King' (l. 285) and draws his sword. There will be moments of stillness and intent scrutiny between the two men that mark the risks involved (see ll. 220–2); Antonio catches Sebastian's words and reuses them. Then, as the focus becomes narrowly intent, Ariel enters with music, speech and song: suddenly the stage is alive again, and Sebastian and Antonio are found with drawn swords and 'ghastly looking' (l. 300). The confusion is thorough: Sebastian now leads in giving information; he tells of 'bellowing' bulls or lions;

Gonzalo has heard a 'humming', Alonso nothing. They all have drawn 'weapons' now (l. 313), but the King still thinks of his son, and Gonzalo of the 'Heavens'; and Ariel, who has been watching, concludes with a satisfied couplet and a reminder that all is safe; he probably leaves in the opposite direction. The '*noise of thunder*' at the start of the next scene follows immediately, threatening godlike anger.

II. ii

If played on a Jacobean stage with two main entrances at either side, Caliban must enter from where the politicians have just made their distracted *exeunt*, or, much less likely, from where Ariel has made his later, pleased *exit*. In either case the deliberate curse gives strong and meaningful contrast; and so will the change in the course of his soliloquy, from insurrection to the fear that makes him 'fall flat' on his own thoughts of 'madness' (l. 14) and on the entry of a fool (l. 15).

Fear turns to comedy with Trinculo's demonstrative soliloquy, which provides opportunities for comic business which will make the audience laugh at him, at Caliban and at the storm itself. Stephano's entry 'comforted' by his bottle and 'scurvy tune'· rides on the comic tide, surmounting even the thought of death (see ll. 41-2), and then the physical comedy of a beast with four legs and two voices, and of a bottle of wine, develops freely as Stephano takes charge of the situation. However fear persists comically, in Trinculo's 'trembling' (l. 76) and Caliban's expectation of torment and, finally, when Stephano hears his own name called and answers with 'Mercy, Mercy!' (l. 90); this comic-serious climax almost parts the comic trio. But recognition leads to elation: dancing for Trinculo (see l. 106) and boasting for Stephano. A surprise development is Caliban's contrasting and affecting aside: 'That's a brave god, . . . I will kneel to him' (ll. 109–10).

It is sometime before Caliban can worship Stephano, for his god is busy mocking Trinculo, and the fool either does not resent or does not even hear (ll. 121-3). When Caliban does make contact, Stephano indulges in the offered fantasy of his own divinity, and at last commands what Caliban has offered: 'Come on, then; down, and swear' (l. 143). Here Stephano's words are direct and insistent, and it is Trinculo who speaks aside; he laughs and he does not understand. Stephano insists again: 'Come, kiss' and then Caliban offers all the riches he knows with delicate and loving detail. Now Stephano is fully King in his own imagination. It is not clear from the punctuation in the Folio (or in the modern editions) exactly what happens next, but either Stephano commands Trinculo to carry the bottle and be butler to his own majesty as he had been to Alonso (the Folio and the natural run of the lines rather support this reading), or else Caliban is made butler and Trinculo, for the time being, ordered to take part in the business of government.

A further change follows, for Caliban now goes wild, singing 'drunkenly', 'howling' and repeatedly crying 'Freedom'; Stephano follows in admiration: 'O brave monster! Lead the way!'

The comic scene, in its passions, servitude, imaginative life, and exercise of power, is closely tied to the preceding action; and its asides, especially those of Caliban and Trinculo, encourage the audience to appreciate the complicated interplay. The song and procession at the end represent the most concerted action yet seen in the play; and all this has come about with no more magic than a thunderstorm at the very beginning of the scene that has passed long before its warm-hearted, strong-voiced and energetic conclusion. The key to the scene is Stephano's bullying and unquestioned assumption of power.

III. i

Ferdinand, bearing logs, forgets his labour in thoughts of his mistress during the opening soliloquy, and again in the course of their encounter.

The emotional range of this short scene is remarkable. Miranda's wishing that the logs had been burnt by lightning is the first sign of a new attitude to her father. With Ferdinand, she shows both modesty and pride, and later both 'bashful cunning' and 'innocence' (ll. 81-2). She confesses the hold Ferdinand has taken over her imagination and at the next moment realises that she prattles 'something too wildly' (ll. 57-8). Ferdinand has not forgotten his grief nor his princely responsibilities, yet in remembering them he counts himself Miranda's 'slave'. She is glad and weeps: she takes initiative and offers herself as wife with simple and directly affecting words. Now they pledge their hands and hearts but, at once, bid farewell. It is not clear why they part so soon: they are almost surely thinking of Prospero's repression and antagonism at their previous meeting (see 'bondage', l. 89), but they do not speak of it. They leave with hearts full of each other.

During all this Prospero is on stage watching. In his first aside he sees their love as a plague providing conventional comedy. By his second he recognises its rarity and prays for blessings on 'that which breeds between 'em'. But in this scene he does not interfere as he had done in I. ii; they are now free. His concluding soliloquy, as the lovers turn from each other, recognises that he cannot equal their glad rejoicing, though nothing could please him more. This self-awareness may lead to a touch of irony as he sends himself back to his magic 'book' (l. 94) and his business; perhaps Ferdinand is still dragging his log off stage.

III. ii

The comic trio returns, divided. Stephano exploits his king-image, fancying himself as heroic athlete and soldier (ll. 11–15). Caliban is drunk and, when he is required to speak, offers to lick his new master's shoe and deprecates Trinculo. Trinculo is content in the enjoyment of folly including his own, until Caliban goads Stephano into threatening him with death (ll. 31–5): at once he is silent, for he is no hero. The scene becomes quiet and static as Caliban kneels, and Stephano stands, with Trinculo in support, as if he were a king giving audience. The drunken 'tottering' (see l. 6) yields to comic solemnity and concentration: Caliban picks his words.

At this point Ariel enters invisible and turns the conspiracy into a game of contradiction and chase. As the physical comedy develops, the involvement of the characters becomes clearer: Stephano becomes more brutal to Trinculo; Trinculo perplexed by Ariel's interference sees more clearly the stupidity of his fellows (ll. 74–8); Caliban asks for punishment for Trinculo and sees himself inflicting it, and then gets to his main purpose. His speech is brutal when forseeing Prospero's death, and then directly expresses his rooted and competitive hatred. To revenge himself through Stephano, he offers Miranda as bait so that his new king shall enjoy that pleasure which had raised his own desire and so brought about his own banishment from Prospero's love (see I. ii. 345–51). The speech breaks through the comedy with sustained and detailed expression of private and unappeased desire.

Ariel is silent until Stephano in imagined success has drawn Trinculo back into the conspiracy. But he serves chiefly to remind the audience of Prospero, and Caliban's pleasure is allowed to grow. Stephano leads the trolling of a catch that, with echoes of many earlier scenes, celebrates both punishment and freedom of thought. The revelry probably mounts quickly but it must end in some kind of confusion, for Caliban succinctly complains: 'That's not the tune.' The right tune played by the invisible Ariel turns comedy into fear; Trinculo panics first—'O, forgive me my sins'—and, after some show of resistance, Stephano follows suit with 'Mercy upon us!' The new king denies being 'afeard', but Caliban recognises fear when he sees it and in a delicate and gently sustained speech comforts his fellows, in the only way he can, with a dream of riches falling from heaven. The placing of this speech is as remarkable as its contents: Alonso, Gonzalo, Antonio, Ferdinand and Miranda have already shown the strength of their imaginary worlds (see, for example, I. ii. 486, II. i. 199–200 and III. i. 56–7); Ariel is about to appear as a harpy from the heavens to the 'men of sin'; Prospero in the next Act will destroy the masque which represents his own 'fancies' and then will liken all reality to a dream. The delight, power and insecurity of imaginary reality is made evident throughout the play. In the fifth Act there is some accommodation with factual and reasonable reality, through solemn music and Prospero's temperate control (see V. i. 58–68, 79–82, 123–5, 153–60, 175–7, 229–30, 295–7). When Prospero invites Alonso and his train to his cell he promises to tell a discourse that will make the night pass quickly—perhaps he here suggests that reality has become like a waking dream.

After Caliban's dream speech, a drunken procession after the invisible taborer soon concludes the scene. The three mortals are sharply contrasted in bearing: Stephano thinks of his kingdom and his own pleasure; Trinculo simply wishes to follow, both the music and someone else who will lead the way: Caliban, notably, thinks nothing of the music or his fellows. After the purposeful 'When Prospero is destroy'd', Caliban silently obeys; Stephano's address to him can serve to focus attention on this silence.

III. iii

As the comics go out, probably singing and shouting the words of their catch—'Thought is free'—the politicians enter the other way, dull, tired and, as asides and grouping on stage soon make clear, divided. Then the first of the island's masques begins without verbal preparation.

Immediate reactions are not unlike those of the comics when they heard the tune of their catch: wonder and fear. But the politicians soon begin to talk, for even amazement can be made familiar by other instances. Prospero, appearing '*on the top, invisible*', has asides that turn the effect of what is said against the speakers. Necessity and convenience lead the politicians to persuade themselves that they should eat, and Prospero's trap has been sprung. However, Alonso's desperation is the last consideration and he draws the others with him.

The theatrical trick of the harpy's appearance will secure attention for his speech, and the madness of the politicians and the control of their swords will ensure that the arraigned are soon as much in view as the figure of vengeance. Direct mention of Prospero and address to Alonso give intensity to the speech before it concludes in a wider view and a short, quiet counterstatement to the main theme of tempest, anger and fate.

The mocking dance and quiet removal of the table to soft music is accompanied by Prospero's calm summing-up, the more impressive for his preceding silence, his lofty position, and the reserved, compact threat of 'They now are in my power.'

The general *exeunt* at the end of the scene is not at all simple. First a 'strange stare' (l. 95) and then a longish speech by Alonso accepting the sea-vision; only as he leaves the stage does it become clear that he has resolved on suicide. Sebastian, this time seconded rather than led by Antonio, rushes out to fight desperately. The natural response of the other courtiers must be to follow, but Gonzalo holds them back for counsel: Adrian's short speech makes it obvious that Gonzalo is hastening what is already taking place, and the counsellor is left to 'follow'.

IV. i

The new Act starts with the formal betrothal 'afore heaven' (l. 7) of Ferdinand and Miranda. This is no casual occasion: it repeats a less formal occasion (see ll. 4–5); it is prefaced by a kind of apology for Prospero's testing of Ferdinand. It is over in nine words, but is followed by a further hint of Prospero's uncertainty ('Do not smile at me . . . '). The need to speak is all Prospero's: Miranda is silent; Ferdinand is briefly assured. When Prospero warns, with ornate physical imagery, against premarital intercourse, Ferdinand answers him more extensively but

with firmly assured syntax and detail. Prospero seems satisfied and leaves
them to talk, but Ariel, entering on his summons, hails a 'potent master'
(l. 34). In Prospero's instructions there is a strange note of strict com-
pulsion: 'I must use you ... Go bring the rabble ... It is my promise ...'.
Ariel's jingle, five times rhymed and ending on a double question: 'Do
you love me, master? No?', suggests that the spirit senses constriction
and lack of ease. (Later he says he had not told Prospero about Caliban
at this time because 'I fear'd Lest I might anger thee', ll. 168–9.) Prospero's
reply is reassuring but dismissive. When he speaks again to the lovers he
repeats his earlier warning, with sharper syntax and more direct attack.
Ferdinand is formal and precise, and Prospero answers with an enigmatic
'Well.' Then he calls for the masque, sharply.

The metre, elaborate address, verbal decoration, godlike behaviour
and, probably, the clear tone of boys' voices and use of stage machinery,
all help to create a contrastingly rich and assured illusion for the masque.
When Iris has reminded her audience of Prospero's warning about 'bed-
right', Juno appears and song follows in octosyllabics with double
rhyme-endings and internal rhymes: Ferdinand describes the 'vision' as
majestic and paradisal.

Curiously, the masque then moves to dumb show as the goddesses
'whisper seriously' (l. 125): this regains precise attention and the hurrying
and holiday-making entries of nymphs and reapers lead to the dance
'toward the end' of which encounter Prospero breaks his own spell.

The significance of this crux has already been discussed several times
in this study. In performance it will be seen as a surprise, a conundrum, a
disturbance of illusion: the whole play founders as a ship at sea. The very
focus is disturbed. Ferdinand and Miranda comment, but do not speak
to Prospero or approach him. When he addresses them it seems that he
has not heard what has been said, and he will further perplex both them
and his theatre audience with talk of the world's dissolution and with an
allusion to the rapid and noisy destruction of the dance as if it had melted
or faded into air. The lovers say nothing, to his reassurance, to his
explanation or philosophy, or to his self-apology. When Prospero dismisses them, their thoughts are not for their own fears or amazement,
but for his peace of mind. Alone he calls Ariel, thanking him before he is
there. The drama is within his mind and being: his fear found in an
image of perfection; his desire to defend, control and punish; his anger

against the irresponsive Caliban and his new, power-struck 'King'.

With Ariel Prospero is direct, precise, attentive and, seemingly, prepared; as if in contrast with thoughts of Caliban, he speaks of his 'spirit' and his 'bird'. Ariel's detailed and amused account of the comic trio contrasts with Prospero's earlier anger and with the more reiterative and self-revealing fury of the soliloquy which then follows the spirit's departure. Probably another revaluation of the situation for the audience comes when, in silence that holds up the action, Ariel, with perhaps Prospero helping, hangs the 'glistering apparel' on the lime tree. Certainly there is a watchful quiet (cf. ll. 194-5 and 205-6) when Caliban and the others enter to the now eavesdropping magician. Prospero is waiting to test these would-be murderers: he seems to insist on freedom now—for them to destroy themselves.

Caliban holds the conspiracy together, with determination and flattery. Because every other course seems fraught with difficulties, Stephano begins to listen and to see himself once more as hero; he offers his hand to Caliban and indulges in 'bloody thoughts'. But, just then, Trinculo sees the clothes and hails Stephano as King: they are trapped. Nothing Caliban can say diverts them from indulging their fantasies. The 'King' at first is silent, then he bullies and, on submission, is gracious. At first the fool accepts that the clothes must be for Stephano, but he helps himself too until directly forbidden; then he gives way subserviently until he rises again with a jest. Stephano is so caught up with the idea of sovereignty that he neglects to use Caliban until Trinculo reminds him, whereupon both jester and butler load the 'monster' with burdens. Caliban's precise (and unavailing) protests contrast with the climax of fantasy success. However, Prospero's spirit-hounds are heard before they are seen: and Caliban, Stephano and Trinculo have nothing more to say or do, but to suffer and 'roar' (l. 260) like beasts.

Prospero's concluding speech is partly soliloquy: the whole play is in his hands; once more he is quiet and in control of all his 'enemies' (l. 263).

V. i

Prospero's entry in his *magic robes* (S.D.) echoes the opening of his first scene.

Ariel's account of the courtiers starts in his usual amused and objective manner, but then focuses on Gonzalo's grief with sustained (by rhythm, image and assonance) delicacy. Perhaps Prospero is romanticising in supposing that Ariel has human feelings, a reflection of his own inner-most, tender affections; in performance some Ariels will almost cry, others will almost taunt their master. But certainly Prospero's 'project' (l. 1) is here governed by his sympathy for others: the brief question and the assurance, 'And mine shall' (ll. 19 and 20) are unique in his relation-ship with his chief spirit, and mark both issue and decision.

The invocation of elves and spirits is delicate and powerful, growing into a full and awesome account of Prospero's power and pride—'rifted Jove's stout oak With his own bolt'; it also claims power over the dead, a feat unnecessary for the narrative of the play but significant in suggest-ing the total hold Prospero has gained over his enemies. The huge transition from 'my so potent art' to 'But this rough magic I here abjure' is not merely in meaning: the rhythm of the whole passage has just reached its culmination and is about to be rebuilt on another basis that issues into the quieter, long phrases of renunciation (ll. 54–7) and then 'Solemn music' (S.D.). The drama here is inward, as after the masque, but controlled and expressed in soliloquy in Prospero's own time and with an impression of deep self-knowledge.

The courtiers, entering silent (with the 'frantic gestures' that echo their departure from Act III) and then standing charmed within a circle, are shown to be puppets at Prospero's disposal; the contrast between these creatures and the magician of the preceding soliloquy is compelling.

The speech that follows is clear, point by point, and grows in per-formance. Prospero must weep; he reserves bitter words for his brother and also the explicit (and determined) 'I do forgive thee'; he is aware of them all, and then prepares himself to be dressed as one of them. His words to Ariel after the robing suggest that he is submitting himself to discipline: 'I shall miss thee, But yet thou shalt have freedom' (ll. 95–6); he is about to resign imaginative delight with the resignation of his power.

The recognition scene is prolonged, so that each member of it is clearly revealed. Gonzalo is the first to regain speech, only to fail to recognise Prospero in an address to heaven. Alonso, while still influenced by 'madness' (l. 116) and wonder, resigns power over the Dukedom and entreats pardon. Sebastian makes a sharp aside; Antonio is notably silent, even when directly and individually addressed. Prospero himself is revealed, embracing Alonso and Gonzalo, as capable of sympathy ('some subtleties o' th' isle'), harshness and some reserve ('to call brother would even infect my mouth'), gentleness and almost playfulness ('I rather think You have not sought her help, of whose soft grace . . . '). He cuts short the recognitions with unequivocal pronouncement ('I am Prospero, and that very duke . . . ') and the discovery of Ferdinand and Miranda.

Miranda's acceptance of Prospero's former enemies as a 'brave new world' (l. 183) is placed for strong contrast; Prospero responds with both understanding and humorous awareness. Gonzalo breaks a long and notable silence to direct attention to the gods, and then a golden (cf. l. 208) and totally optimistic account of what has happened; it is notable, and in performance very noticeable, that no one else actively echoes his sentiments. After his 'Amen', it is Gonzalo himself who first sees the Master and Bosun and, with unchanged character, prides himself on his percipiency.

With the Bosun's account of the wreck and deliverance, the conclusion of the play gains something of a comic impetus, but also re-establishes the dream-like perspective and reminds the stage and theatre audiences of Prospero's former power over man's imagination and senses. The rapid entry of Stephano, Trinculo and Caliban continues these impressions, and reflects further on the characters already assembled. Sebastian and Antonio (now breaking a long silence) can use them for comic exploitation (ll. 263–6), but Prospero emphasises danger (ll. 268–274) and, having gained attention, insists on responsibility:

> Two of these fellows you
> Must know and own; this thing of darkness I
> Acknowledge mine. (ll. 274–6)

Caliban's reactions are picked out by Shakespeare's handling of the scene: his fear in immediate response ('I shall be pinch'd to death') and then, when Alonso redirects attention to his ensuing silence, his determination to 'seek for grace' (l. 295)—that essential which Prospero has said can never be his (cf. IV. i. 188–92). Caliban's verbal contribution to the last scene is small, but it has huge implications, starting with a private cry to 'Setebos', his witch-mother's god, and then a recognition of wonder rapidly turning to fear. Finally, he has to see himself for the first time as a 'thrice-double ass' and at once submit to a curt order. Each actor of Caliban will find his own way of giving meaning to this silent exit by physical performance: it might be triumph over the fools, or defeat of his hopes, or incomprehension, or a quiet acceptance of proper slavery, or a dawning freedom and patience, or something of all this. And each audience will give the *exit* close attention: it will have been held by Caliban's sensitivity and impressed by his superiority over his fellow conspirators in determination and resource; above all it will have recognised so clearly the pressure of thwarted love and pride in his murderous hatred of Prospero that some may believe him wronged, that following his instincts and trying to rape Miranda did not deserve this degree of degradation. Prospero had remembered Caliban when indulging his dearest fancies of a world reborn (see page 42, above), and Shakespeare's handling of his last appearance and this last *exit*, refusing both sentimental and moral smoothness to the working out of Caliban's part in the play and refusing a clear verbal statement, encourages the audience to remember him too: the audience must meet the actor in understanding, responding in imagination. Caliban has been realised with intensity and immediacy; he is Prospero's short-loved subject, his failure, disturbance, responsibility; he represents the turbulence of human nature encountered outside ourselves and becoming part of ourselves, part of our own inner tempest.

Alonso's and Sebastian's words and the *exeunt* of Stephano and Trinculo along with Caliban (now both under his command) help to hold and elaborate this largely non-verbal and ambiguous moment of Caliban's dismissal. The irresponsible and yet imaginative insurrection of 'King Stephano' and his followers has this topsy-turvy, bewildered outcome when it submits to Prospero's clear-eyed judgement: it is pathetic, comic, incidental, unfinished.

Prospero concludes the play, drawing attention forward to subsequent events and relating events to his own consciousness. Then at the last possible moment he releases Ariel. Presumably the others are 'spell-stopped' for this exchange; certainly they are unmoving, for the next words invite them to 'draw near'. In awareness and in speed Ariel's exit must make a strong contrast; a pause will sharpen the audience's appreciation of Ariel's failure to respond except with flight and pleasure, and of Prospero's feelings of affection and regret, and possibly his hope for gain from loss. This concluding moment has considerable ambiguity, in silence, for the presentation of both servant and master. And it gives to

Prospero's four concluding words—'Please you, draw near'—great subtextual implications of final, considered acceptance of his fellow human-beings.

Epilogue

The octosyllabics, the isolated figure on the stage, the change of resonance will compel close attention and allow a slow pace. The relation of audience to speaker (who remains, persistently, 'in character') is also totally new and unexpected: the man of power, imagination and mercy had risked loneliness and rejection. Also new and still more unexpected is the word 'despair', which Prospero had never recognised within himself throughout the play and which his very name seems to deny: even the acceptances of the last Act had been poised on a precipice of hopelessness.

The following reference to 'prayer', the sharpness of 'pierce', and the reflection in 'Mercy' and 'free' of so many crises in the play itself, together with the allusion to the Lord's prayer, all widen the scope of Prospero's epilogue and prepare for the direct challenge of the last couplet, in which 'crimes' and 'indulgence' cast the widest net and direct the most particular appeal to the audience. After a good performance of the play, the audience's applause is an act of identification that cannot be easy, an affirmation of hope against the most carefully wrought despair. Acknowledging the art of the actor and the dramatist, each member of the audience will be aware of his own role outside the theatre.

5. Acknowledgements and Reading Guide

Immediately before writing this book, I directed a production of *The Tempest* for the Department of Drama and Theatre Arts of Birmingham University that was shown at the Crescent Theatre, Birmingham, in October 1967; I am greatly indebted to the cast and my other collaborators. I was subsequently helped in clarifying my view of the play by discussions with the graduate seminar of Munich University; I am very grateful to Professor W. H. Clemen for the stimulation of this visit.

Among many books about *The Tempest*, four have been especially useful in my studies, and while gratefully acknowledging their help I would recommend them to other students. Frank Kermode's Arden Edition (1954) annotates the text with care and learning, reprints selections from the sources and the original music and, in the introduction, places the work in a wide literary perspective. R. H. West, *The Invisible World* (1939) and W. C. Curry, *Shakespeare's Philosophical Patterns* (1936) usefully document and comment upon the supernatural elements of the play. A reading of Enid Welsford's *The Court Masque* (1927) is the first requirement for a historical appreciation of the 'shows' or 'revels' within the play.

On the original staging, two *Shakespeare Association Pamphlets* are to be recommended: J. Isaacs, 'Production and Stage Management at the Blackfriars Theatre' (1933) and E. Law, 'Shakespeare's *Tempest* as originally produced at Court' (1920). The basic facts of later stage-history are to be found in the *New Cambridge Shakespeare*, ed. J. D. Wilson (1921); a full history of *The Tempest* in the theatre is yet to be written.

More extensive reprints of the Bermuda reports are to be found in *The Elizabethans' America*, ed. L. B. Wright, *Stratford-upon-Avon Library, 2* (1965), together with many other documents and publications about the New World.

Textual problems may most profitably be studied in relation to those of other Shakespeare plays in W. W. Greg, *The Shakespeare First Folio.* (1955).

Twentieth-century criticism of *The Tempest* and other 'last plays' or romances is reviewed by Philip Edwards in *Shakespeare Survey*, xi (1958). Contrasting and stimulating studies are to be found in G. W. Knight, *The Shakespearian Tempest* (1932); D. G. James, *Scepticism and Poetry* (1937); E. M. W. Tillyard, *Shakespeare's Last Plays* (1938); F. R. Leavis, *The Common Pursuit* (1942); Clifford Leech, *Shakespeare's Tragedies and other Studies in Seventeenth-Century Drama* (1950); J. F. Danby, *Poets on Fortune's Hill* (1952); Derek Traversi, *Shakespeare: The Last Phase* (1954); David William, '*The Tempest* on the Stage', *Stratford-upon-Avon Studies, 1: Jacobean Theatre* (1960); Jan Kott, *Shakespeare, Our Contemporary* (tr. 1964); A. D. Nuttall, *Two Concepts of Allegory: A Study of Shakespeare's 'The Tempest' and the Logic of Allegorical Expression* (1967); Anne Righter, Introduction, *New Penguin Shakespeare* (1968); R. A. Foakes, *Shakespeare: The Dark Comedies to the Last Plays* (1971); F. A. Yates, *Shakespeare's Last Plays: A New Approach* (1975). *Later Shakespeare* (Stratford-upon-Avon Studies 8 (1968), ed. J. R. Brown and B. Harris, contains several essays of interest to students of *The Tempest*, including S. W. Wells on 'Shakespeare and Romance' and J. P. Brockbank on 'Conventions of Art and Empire' in the play.

W. H. Auden's series of poems called 'The Sea and the Mirror: A Commentary on Shakespeare's *The Tempest*' and published in *For the Time Being* (1945) is memorable for its own sake and for its reflection of Shakespeare's play.

All quotations and references in this book are from Shakespeare, *Complete Works*, ed. P. Alexander (1951).

Selected Index

Milton, John
  L'Allegro, 21
Mirandola, Pico della, 16
Montaigne, Michel Eyquem de,
  Essays, tr. J. Florio, 15

Nashe, Thomas, 24–5
New World, The, 16–17

Ovid
  Metamorphoses, tr. A. Golding,
  15
Pembroke, Earl of, 17
Petrarch, 20
Plotinus, 15
Plutarch
  Lives, tr. Sir Thomas North, 14

Revels, see Masques

Sermon on the Mount, The, 16
Shakespeare, Anne, 12
Shakespeare, Judith, 12
Shakespeare, William
  Antony and Cleopatra, 11, 42 n.
  As You Like It, 19, 20, 22, 48
  Cardenio, 12
  Comedy of Errors, The, 42 n.
  Coriolanus, 11, 18
  Cymbeline, 11, 19, 20, 38
  Hamlet, 11, 18, 20, 38, 41
  Henry V, 20
  I, Henry VI, 42 n.
  III, Henry VI, 23
  Henry VIII, 12
  King Lear, 11, 20, 38, 42 n.
  Love's Labour's Lost, 20

Macbeth, 11, 19, 42 n.
Measure for Measure, 19, 25–6
Merchant of Venice, The, 19
Midsummer Night's Dream, A, 19,
  20
Much Ado About Nothing, 19,
  42 n.
Othello, 23–4
Pericles, 11, 19, 24, 38
Richard II, 18
Romeo and Juliet, 11, 42 n.
Sonnets, 13
Taming of the Shrew, The, 42 n.
Tempest, The, passim
Timon of Athens, 11, 42 n.
Titus Andronicus, 21–2, 23
Two Gentlemen of Verona, The,
  22
Two Noble Kinsmen, The, 12
Winter's Tale, The, 9, 11, 18, 19,
  20, 24, 28, 38
Comedies, Histories and Tragedies
  (1623), 10–11, 12
Sidney, Sir Philip
  Arcadia, 15, 21
Smith, John, 17
Southampton, Earl of, 17
Spenser, Edmund
  Faerie Queene, The, 15, 20, 21
Strachey, William, 17

Virgil
  Aeneid, 15, 33

Webster, John
  Duchess of Malfi, The, 35
Whitehall, 9–10, 16